Corey Wakeling | Goad Omen

AF584411

New Poems

GIRAMONDO POETS

Corey Wakeling | Goad Omen

First published 2013
from the Writing & Society Research Centre
at the University of Western Sydney
by the Giramondo Publishing Company
PO Box 752 Artarmon NSW 1570 Australia
www.giramondopublishing.com

© Corey Wakeling 2013

Designed by Harry Williamson
Typeset by Andrew Davies
in 10/16.5 pt Baskerville

Printed and bound by Ligare
Distributed in Australia by NewSouth Books

National Library of Australia
Cataloguing-in-Publication data:

Wakeling, Corey 1985–
Goad Omen / Corey Wakeling
ISBN 9781922146267 (pbk)

A821.3

All rights reserved.
No part of this publication may be
reproduced, stored in a retrieval system
or transmitted in any form or by any means
electronic, mechanical, photocopying or
otherwise without the prior permission of
the publisher.

for my mother and father

Acknowledgements

These poems have appeared in *The Age, The Black Rider, Cordite, The Disappearing (Red Room Company), E-Ratio, ETZ, Five Poetry Journal, foam:e, fourW Anthology 23 (2012), Handsome Journal, Island, Jacket2, nthposition, Overland, Otoliths, Shampoo, Shearsman Magazine,* and *Spork Press*. Some of these poems also appear in the Vagabond Press chapbook *Gargantuan Terrier, Buggy or Dinghy* (2012).

I am indebted to the editors and publishers of the journals, newspapers and anthologies that appear above, and to those who have published work of mine that do not. Thanks to Duncan Hose for permission to use his spectacular painting 'Geronimo', and to Nicholas Walton-Healey for his photographic expertise. Special thanks to Michael Farrell and Gig Ryan for valuable advice on drafts of *Goad Omen*. Finally, thank you to K.O., for devoted support.

This project has been assisted by the Commonwealth Government through the Australia Council, its arts funding and advisory body.

Contents

Dennis Hopper is Dead

The American Returns to Rottnest

the jade American with a thick face
before he returns to bivouac with the quokkas

Webb has a silent poem about the island
'all the sea like a stylus'

an uncle, the greater Darling Ranges, has overseen
the worthy effort of barbecue smelt, respite from
the derelict tennis court called the tennis court derelict

The to and fro spectated as we were by the cannons
of the silent star jumps in journalese,
like the mettle of pig flesh, anyhow I left forever the moment
she throttled that chihuahua

Is that dash from the murder of the chihuahua
behind me? Where once I had access to the intimate
novels, swimming in her pools of ink, now I grovel
like cracks in the intercom

The jarrahs are much within, and, nearby,
the hierarchy of kookaburras
Fate is somewhat similar to the son of the physiotherapist,
a bushranger's shot at a crossroads of commercial traffic

Is it that they're able to see the glint of the polished?
No, the absence of the hand of fate is temporal
this crossroads in the suburban castle at sight of the horizon's city,
the novelist

However, the vision was the American's, whose bloodless cheeks
gad about the old barracks

Having answered the Sphinx's kōan with an un-stringed
racket, the view thus the crossroads requite entry into fate

But fate cannot, the Cessna is dead, and the parlour of blue
is intact

Hear the fusillades, the powder éclat
of the seventeenth century gluey,
the anarchic and gutless rove
of a crass hermeneutics of genealogy

Archipelago Cantilever

True, the fir copses and snow tops beyond
the accountant of mourning enlists
the dolorous glamour of today, be she who reposes
on the bed of softest needles in imaginary
talks with the mouth of all accounts, or flocculent
in the territories where sex diffuses, nearby planet greenback.
Grey presence near the terrace at dawn with a Dictaphone.
The pate of science's love of its son, *The Castle* in reverse,
protagonist teething, the apostate prophet.
This greenback turns pink in the wash.
Folkloric, the Cossack-like franchise city square
where Latin dwindles and missiles bilge, having sold
dollars for dollars and junks.

If I were to wear a tent, where would my skull be?
Amplitude is the redaction of the historic noble
from the banknote, inviting junks to its mortar,
sorry peninsula of rusted out tankers
and the unpopulated islands. Might the village
be equated with a hole in the heart, polka
entreats? Patiently sober, science's son swinging
from the trapeze of the hairlessness of mourning,
one of ten competitors mousey. Have you ever seen so much skin
on an owl, and so obnoxious?
Must have been brutalised when the territories shed
and made that bed of soft needles.

Not altogether strange franchised, all the floating
junks about the islands surrounding village
Heart Stop.

Tent land Australia, impasto stone bridge in lieu
of filigrees of the gilded fall of angels,
un-verdant aluminium palanquin of which
a lathe shapes a hot rod,
fusion promise and analysand,
in the wash turns pink but soaked in sun's bleach
and yellows like the shattering iris.
Even the yawn of a sad mouth is a sob.

A Bull Crushing Steam at the Tomb of the Unknown Poet

after Gig Ryan's 'That laments'

He has been sent to Lake Como to attend a pit fight staged
by an insurance broker from Melbourne. When peninsulas
are ranges, and seas are dialects away, the bull
is treated to paintings and olives before a fight. Of nothing
he thinks all day.
Speleology, he enters, forgetting a short life
        of theatre.
A lesser-known matador anonymous wanders into the cave
to encounter the napping bull, cuts a lock of the mane, ties it
to the buckle of his belt for good. On the walls of the unlit,
of which the bull pays no attention, ideographs
of the hunt. They are of redness where he is blackness. Like night,
when the mountains carry mist but no man. Midnight itinerants
of Como make their own way into the lake
without recourse to surface. Tomorrow morning, the bull learns
his odds. The picadors join the festivities, but participate only
in the beer drinking. Bull knows the Melburnian's name,
not his opponent's. Unlike Barcelona's *Plaza de Toros*,
the bull will not leave clouds of dust.
Instead, like a dreamer, he will crush the mist.

My Hounds

My hounds will never find me,
even with cracks in the tabula rasa.
After all, they have
the lyrebird to discover.
It will be the Yarra today
and for all of tomorrow,
though the hawthorn has otherwise
captivated love,
though no passage seems to proceed thence.
I wasn't born here, hereby Yarra, brown and glossy.
The statuary province of Charles George Gordon
Exhibition et al. might bear a basking irrelevance, but hats
betray our vagrancy by the Yarra. We sit awhile.
The hounds will never find me, my hounds
or otherwise, the Yarra yellowing
like a similarly withering dandelion
overshadowed by the best red gum.
She takes pictures of canoes and freshmen,
is otherwise captivated by the hawthorn.
Princes Bridge outlines the prevailing picture of surveillance
and skullcaps, providing the lectern and rostrum to a city
proscenium.
What
emptiness!
Still absent. It must be the wigs and the gathered yokes and
the black coats the hounds are in thrall of,
then.

The Suburbs

He wades darkly through the marshlands,
out to the fallow semaphore, but on nabbing it
is burnt from his clasp, by this discovers its
watery indifference, red and persistent.
He's to return handless, or empty to the clamps
and limbs of the car manufacturer,
he forgets which, many suburbs and marshlands thence.
It'd ruin him to resemble the black bear,
but it's the black bear forces itself on him, until
they are dead,
tread the water unconscious.
They go up and down, round and around,
through and beneath the reeds and juvenile
toads. Attended by the avoirdupois of the black bear
bears gravitas, means he is not afraid
as he would have been heeding the eastern European
scaffolder composer's fable, Janáček, swift utility
in the unfortunate hands of an Alaskan, and so forth.

Koalas stay seated, paw on breast and face in belly,
bliss of bunking with one's larder.
Abandoned daisy in the glade, fears of the Seine
breaststroker quashed as boy and beast
penetrate the bushland, preserve the slow Sturt peas,
their secret predation in the sand piles amid

the scrub above the marshes. Back to the suburb of squats,
the boy says, the beast purring but otherwise unspoken.
The bear's mother had sung the same melody of marshland
penetration when he'd been a cub. The bear had sung
with its devil alongside him, since it matters not whether
you're beast or boy black bristles of the return
through dimness with only the semaphore fomenting
hearts of the boys who would walk the perimeters
of their suburbs, spit blue ash as they rub against one another.

If only I was slower than a starfish, boy thinks. Otherwise,
the tunnel of locomotion and the blue sparks of night
and enforcement of extempore orienteering shrink him,
the bloated grimace.

Beast will never betray to boy the verbatim lyric as they together
grow defiant, verboten passage recalling them
to the red beacon tucked within the reeds.

The Renaissance

The better part of a plotting fulcrum joined to the bean spasms
of all these futurists, I kiss your nipples and run soap nails
like a death-row comb through your hair.
The Mussolini balcony *in situ* swelters like swine crackling,
wreaths of rosemary do nothing to transform pig's head.
Rome did protest its masquerade of pork,
plus goat shins, though not to entertain the depths
of the apartment tenancy which swallows all
fondness for buried parchments. May the magpie
eat the tenant ideograms of the leadlights glowing limen-lit.

I kiss the only soft part of you, the belly, and touch
the refusal spot, thence collapse of the rhododendron
and the bougainvillea
of the aesthetics of the Renaissance.

I see carabanieri turning their berets in the reverse,
in remembrance of their leviathan swallowed by an offshore vortex.
The rat's head ocarina whistles like your grit teeth,
face red and green behind the leadlight
of a mallee gum copse, and in Bacchus Marsh I am in retreat.
One under thus city bound, the king floats like a cretin ghost
citing the call numbers to the histories of secret smugglers,
thus I love the Korean libraries earthquake droned and fall in love
with your immaculate teeth and your eyes of mother-of-pearl.

The coup of murals and the plague of rats,
the coo of the rat ocarina and the formal woman
presented as vellum for the single Chinese character: 愛
There is to be no ceiling, but an avenue of basements,
and invitations come in call numbers.
The library at Otaru served sake from an ideogram barrel
between which no rat subsists, since the hay
of their packages is gone, perished. Bad seasons.
There's no forgetting the lull
in visitors when we lay beside each other amongst
lived hardbacks and ink stains and rob the corner
of a quidam's writing room.

The Blush

Not having seen a face in the figure, the taxi rank
auto-annihilates. Fires start about tar not dry thus inflammable.
It's the quiet of gull these moments in comparison
to the ever-clucking pigeon that mules the wet soot
further inland toward the lotus. Melodic interior monologue
salves the face strips the frieze and unmuffles the blush.

Driest anniversary of roaming, the fires loom unassisted
by comeuppance wavering depthless, but eyes shimmer
pace the percussion of patience though lotus guarantee
banquet the animosity hoax, misplacement. Pert nark.
The lounge room the only witness to the squint. The squint
the only witness to tar alight. About now, the tonguing of melody
made scold, sea air muted 'behind the larches'.
Never knew such blushing morning lit, palms black
with the readiness to return. Proof.

Impersonator

Amid suburbs of Melbourne there is a mission for those who scramble by bouleversement, not Catholic. Something Presbyterian, songs ebb. I would lookalike and advance guard from the cottage reticula, but of the vista and North Melbourne remains the bitten nails of apprenticeships interrogated, so little welcome on the quay, in the channel, through the drainage. Line and lines outbound from oily cess and the untold power coupler of elm and possum carcass. Forgive this return, the ashes lived under give allergies begging explanation. Brick smokestacks do not pet the panther lest woken, and Ned Kelly lookalikes, cheeks of sunset, tin and rivets.
Very best marionette, but takes more than dollars.
Like Ned Kelly lookalikes the horses of jaunty children
and the secular pageant of dark ponies of fresh homes loosening
sheet metal from and scavenging through darkened night,
little voices subscribe orison in colour to the vigil of the slumberous
fountain. Just be sure there's something to get his teeth into.
Embarrassed! even the eyes colour red. Look at you.
A coastal paperbark, swooning golden cheek to sandy ground
you past bedtime geezer.

Whose genius led you to strip the verandahs of townhouses,
choke the frangipanis,
Whose force fashions homes into costumes of the antediluvian,
Pre-Socratic steeled and sunset of cheeks, abashments of the flint
stones of congregation and its cocked skeleton of the compass
white gum? Who but Nolan impersonator hallway proletariat,

not knoll glum with saucy invention chalked onto slate, reader,
for all conspicuousness,
to build your startling retreat on, advance guard dispersal fornicating
like the hurricane of wild ponies. Flattering, the voice in the hall!

That impersonating genius has led you to further
accomplishment considering the weekend apprenticeship,
of cooked jarrahwood clinging to the heirloom suits
of adopted strangers, though their wet whispers
cool the embarrassment of the bare skulls you've opened.
Yes, your dream with a redback inside is gilt love.

Current Affairs

for 'A flood of fountain-foam'
Alfred Lord Tennyson 'The Palace of Art'

Marvellous news for all: we get box seats,
theses precede us. Smoking room mid-levitation
visits the prone brain, whilst the fast one fastens
Sibyl Vane, the name in spades wherewithal,
destined for Jocastaesque skit by Elizabeth Malet.

The theses drag out applause, begin with encore
set including languorous, sympathetic waves, intermission
Yokozuna Hakuhō versus Baruto, close with birth.
We're parched by cigar smoke but feel good enough.
Hose ignites a parasol, nothing singed bar
the organ grimoire. Yes, each key is a glyph
to the recombinant Song of the Dead, its brass
music box scroll the entire inventory of porcelain held
by the Andy Warhol estate. Ashen, we feel even better.

Bitter drives soaks, the velvet purse wading gets
its coxcomb, its public caresses, the coastline's apostles skittle.
If the Irish art is 'the cracked looking-glass of the peasant',
dappled usherdom the middle purgatory.
Makes great charcoal cosmetics though, all these cud
cigars the spit leavings Southbank discharges,

Yarra sober elegant. Farrell and Hile fold Vane
into a murder. Footy takes poison. Dad rises agued.
Box Seat Liquefaction the Spartan signs its name
with all the other noms de guerre
scratched into formidable Bath sandstone,
like rasps of the newly animate.

The Swan River

We begin to question they'd make much of us in Bassendean
by the wan ghost gum turned from us face in hands like a war
widow, but all eyes draft Ararat for the incumbent.
The griddle spits canola oil and begs the eye douche, but
James and Carol, who spins the bottle for them? And would your
weapon chosen be a long neck? I nudge you but you leave yours
for congratulations, sweepstakes, penetration of the jungle but
another matchstick of the stochastic that I cannot but let you win,
whoever I am in this memorial at Marienbad.
Livid is the amorous intent of the hedge gardener and his team
of apprentices, see their I-Spy game curdle with jealousy,
their bare toes on the rungs of the bamboo ladders and their hands
throttling the barbed follicles, having caught sight of us.
The graven, they ask questions more abstruse than visa intercourse,
more inclined to toss coins than dice roll. The Bassendean days
are empty but jagged with intent. The old name their statue
after a malingering corpse of the cudgelled sand track, and does
the paint factory brighten? No, turned in grey from the city,
trammelled with blue pallets. The day is as empty as the forklift's
cells, so its driver will bathe his head in the sewer flue.
The wedding of jealousy on the bridge
is traditional, the profligate elderly do not name what is alive.
The forklift driver curses the unnamed. More ubiquitous than
you'd think the ghost gum, swollen in face and tread, living apart
in blossom.

The only supervisors of the Tonkin, red and inflamed, they've loaded their stakes like loading a rifle. And they see the boys disappear on the sandtrack toward nowhere, bush enclosed, having crossed the Swan already. It never forgets.

Cryptomeria

Far more cryptomnesia these days, may it
be born then in the chrysalis
of remembrances, the good forgetting forgotten
running his hands through Akita fur

of acres of shivering fibrillating vice figures
of the iodine-poisoned anodised, glade lain in a country
of cryptomeria.

For the Layperson

Doxa the fossick Protestant as fuck. Epigrams to days
not made yet, but yours before mine.
All these Lincoln beards with revolvers in them. At least I died
going off, you might say. The forefathers so ready
to redact appearing the swingers couple at your own assassination
as beast beset final destination, Two Backs.
Layperson concession, mark the hosiery donned for forcible union
flinch, for how could any flinch be inopportune
auditioning for a bit part in the event
of vocation's redemption. Bourke Street sea of persons.
What clamour at the sprocket. How propose flinch be unreal:
indulge this spat, it is time kindled and the sum of our denim:

spirit with ponytail pacing this post-war lounge divagation,
just give me two years. Give me my kidnap,
if I'm ever to be revolver that redeems me. Moonee Ponds
rote console once the narrative Bildung ist Roman.
Remorse being national sustain, songs of dun din. Bit part
for the party and we together betroth dual evacuee.

Caesars, we illustrate each other by theatre
of torchlight. Earl of Rochester the gun in her shoe.
Their make out is an abomination where the fire fight
is lark song and the treacheries. Nostrum, the mystery plays
are soon replaced with the treacheries. Succour, follow.

The Couples

She can feel the sunburn as it comes on,
better than I can. Something to do with being suspicious
of grinning cacophonists, the sulphur-crested cockatoos.
The forehead's upward glance spurned during the espial,
scorned. Even with all of the gums and the ferns prehistoric
and the felicity of familiar discreetness, fated to the circumspection
of sideways sauntering rosella.
Never mind the other, with the horn no matter how devastating
the heat. Already coupled. One after reiterating the couple
horrisonous. Another, the pursuit, gossamered with yarn.
That sounds like the conversations on insatiable
appetites, the welcoming seat a moistened towel,
it could be dusk is it so blue on a false Belgrave concourse.
Unlike the wide lens of the Southern Hemisphere,
her hands never catch sight of fire in the dry. The head begins blue
turns red. She believes so, at least, impersonating the rosella again.
These are wont to the vaguest predictions, plane tree skiving,

modern politics, black shirts about sulphurous sewers.
Violent bate to the cockatoo's loiter about the blue skip
in groups no cause for alarm. Even cute,
something intoxicated about their white dolling sopor
and the behaviour of eyes perched like glaucoma in muck,
dun, disseminating us as we passed.

Glasgow

Glasgow's pleasurable this time of year,
say the thoughts of the bosom on't.
Too many doves, rafts shatter like bone
dice on the pinnacles awaiting the
sorry hero. If only he had gone like that, but
no, he went like a mouthful of bread, soggy,
insufficient, and atavistic. There is that
Trojan expression, roughly: 'the sons are

not to go like their fathers.' What does
that mean this sunny Glaswegian day, when
all the invisible hawthorns garland the
pleasure wrought of vicarious nostalgia?
What with the student body fulminating, gadding
in cameo appearances, like in a warren,
the children enslaving parent suburbs with pillories,
then dragging them toward their antres,
like childhood, and life illustration.

It would be wiser to close this chapter as if
a periodical, letting Fantômas tear the string of pearls from
a woman's neck, to return to a rightful place, like
rose water myth.

No One

In Western Australia, the desire to come to know
the no one develops as the xanthorrea
incision lodes. The Zig Zag was a railroad is a trek
into the east. Find pink orchids and other invisibles.
Knowing no one, the known washes its hair
in the weir the day it overflows.

Today, we can call it Mundaring, the weir.
Today, you wash your hair. Tomorrow,

you begin the walk again. The banksia cones
are torches are club fists. Thump the one known
with the club fist torch of the banksia till
it perishes the unknown. The weir has lost its body,
is yet still there, kangaroo scat on the breeze
like a public toilet on the Champs-Élysées,
says Marcel, though not to me, says the hunted haunted
West Australia now a car park.
That's what the old folk say. They replaced our town
with a municipal rust cloud of no one.

Mount Difficult

Tomorrow, I promise to find the black boot,
but until then the swine is to be curled up like
a nude. Our mess cloys us. Look up,
the red totems of the Grampians.
Every furrow sprouts mallee and silvery gum,
but footsteps of others pursue us.
Let my espionage look something like this:
the Pyrenees of France and Spain fleeing
the Pyrenees of Victoria, sprouting mallee and silvery gum,
the mauled kangaroo evidence the forage
through our pamphlets, and you and I dashing
for the bluff's cove.

I ask him about the wood stove reaching for a
compartment of white heat, but Mount Difficult hovers
like a prison bunk and I am paralysed.
Its eaves recall the protrusion of the strip mall of Maebashi
and its mountain Akagi, dry as daylight, its foot candescent
green verdigris. I ask him again of the wood stove. There
is something about silicon in my mother's hometown
alight. There is something about haloes of white light
plucked as crowns. No, there is something about
haloes of white light, plucked halogen heaters in the outdoors.

Do we eat pig's head as the cold drops to foolishness?
If I had the right shoes, I'd wander down the street glad
as a madman, but I don't have the smarts, you hear!

The Ox

So free and easy on the draw capital gain
during the years of the ox, when the five-year-old
painted the domestic and spilled your whiskey,
Kazan scapegoat,
you scholar of all three versions of progress.
That pillow book is your surgeon's,
by it family history stretches, like gum,
for some boy-child precocity to pop, no doubt.

At Batman Park, a dance of surfactants about
the tobacco smoke and a small bonfire with molten lead,
like old folks at home in Grafton,
a lung test if you've tried anything like Yeats' symbology
and turned out an architect. Nothing doing, no.
The best known name in Newark versus
unbeaten fuselage-like Hoddle Bridge, strangers
we hallucinate a hanging from the Victorian pommel
lanterns that colour syrup on our return
back, the Yarra near black.

Still, whose municipality for which poverty is numbed
by surgeon's proletarian sacrifice, Batman Park
the gallows a burst in anyone's careerism, old folk pending.
So sways the ox family.

Sanitarium Sanatorium

Wisdom found no place where she could dwell, and her dwelling was in heaven. Wisdom went out in order to dwell among the sons of men, but did not find a dwelling; wisdom returned to her place and took her seat in the midst of the angels.
from *The Ethiopic Book of Enoch* 42, 1–2

'The road of excess' the codicil is a stolen thing, see unfinished
    Enoch,
a book or iceberg. We shiver.
I should think as she turns from us the plummeting seraphim
she somehow looks all the way through us, into that unribbed cage
    of office,
security as baulk; I should think she whispers to herself
'to say *heaven* would induce praise, but to say *never*
would induce parades' as from a woman's womb her ribs
the hand penetrates

Deported from us umbilicus, peace of merchant trade
on scales of presentability, mothers and grandmothers.
Colloquium displayed with the namesake orbits at eyes
and around throats. Like arraignment, in uniformity. Like an arm.
A lull in spasm in comparison condones the punishable.
No undoing irreverent death of the death mask wearer dead
now getting his swathes of honey plaster.

You and I, abacus, ox astride we are not in ordeal but astride another
clambering up the totem scarified and prelapsarian, yes,
at least to get better gist of the air, if contritely.
Of contrition, present your scurry to empty lots by hand with fist,
hands out like hallucination in Tavistock unfinished, hands smarting
after cohort calumny cavort for the weird blue eye
of the mountain, where Tavistock is a book, and chaffed.

Having turned gold on my arrival among flagellant holy –
where is the gold amongst the red, solar? – the gravestone
car yard takes that proneness of supine best, and shimmers
in its polish the glamour of night.
'What a fellowship, what a joy divine, leaning on the everlasting
arms,' Robert Mitchum moaning darkness deep
as bayou protectorate, rogue shotgun. Where now ungainly,
quiet flick knives of eucalyptus celebrating tower impregnable.

Weeping habitus: cachinnation as aubade? In waterside gloom?
Where is asking, begging, the beggared asking, and do the arms,
everlasting?
Do they divinity, do they fellowship? Where is the beggared, the
arms, the arms begging?
Whosoever forgets the condition sterile laps at beck of coke from
burn off, portmanteau for the clasps briefcase recited.
So Abbotsford bound in hessian. The ladder, and the ladders
winding.

Soured then for he whose pastor racks the sanatorium
dredges the sanitarium from the Lego intrigue of final childhood,
where Madonna meets the bog. The story of an eye. Why is it
we call it the swamp, where delicate reverend on the flagstones
sighs spent? Another's Christmas and the Newtown cemetery,
not just he and I driven, scampering like the lambent rats,
and not the fat rats of dope.

Open the blistering desert, cauldron. Glad to finally meet you,
to know you, fox hunt, you lout.
Intentions to set the paralegal to work on the date of another
armistice, to lay down weapons and shake hands, our flags
beating the coolly mannered like the concealed bodhrán.
Some pray to percussion, either way entrenched with fires above
and on all sides. Good. The handshakes sun dried to an integument
like the proper cauterised,

the car crash forced the moment of ironised peace,
percussion of patience, into fascism. For that then no recalcitrance
for Heraclitus, Harvard graduate and favourite, I am speaking
to you now; like you said, easy vote for the vaunt that knows now
is now otherwise, otherwise being a less consequential ria
to what is diversity.
Though it might sculpt all the crags about, here in the Hiroshima
archipelago, it didn't appear to you to be so beforehand;

how about the behindhand stakes? My roll.
Not quite inconsequential, but it wouldn't be the first time

children took their hometown for granted, be made to adapt
the copper to cufflinks for the national effort,
and cauterise the mortified. More orbits go faster. Go faster.
The fastest car's fate near saviour, river spume lathe
cuts all horizons. Apex encountered, bend looming, begging.
        Repeat.
Repeat the kōan that stings, hands of the apex,

the knuckles greying, you leading,
repeat the kōan
that stings, that

'leads to the palace of wisdom'.

There are Deserts in the Human

These days we are rent and your hands
festoon to the sentry, a day officer
whose eyes scour an inner integument,
our verso of scutes, the planetarium.
My hands are in these and you are wanting
hands more. I'm wondering how to give
the planetarium or satellite variable.
That matador and his swollen groin.
There are humans in the desert.
There are deserts in the human, the groin
of the Snowy Mountains like
the prodigal philosopher's festoon,
which is a buggy or dinghy, whichever inland sea
was chosen for scientific despondency.
That variable of you in the shed with the bear trap,
that variable of you in the shed with the secateurs,
that variable of you in recline on a welder's bench
still animated as solder. That'd be farfetched,
or at least a great false augur, Cleopatra
not colonised, whose viper bite remains our only sacrifice,
quanta, laneway possum
dashing its brains beyond the cameras like
a forklift. This means the hill cadenza overseeing
baulks or dazzles as a master, the shed then
a groin, swollen brown with clinamen
splintering on the surface, junction

which all the regional possums call home
not a student fallen stricken, succumbed
Narcissus-ashen murk-gripped, sometimes
truly a wetland of needles. The hills master
a coolabah shed, the tourist we killed wandered
past it, like a tourist, or olive branch,
and if only reticulation could replace the breathlessness
of torso of the swelling landmass.
The hill is neither pitch nor estate, beginning
barren from recent tilling, though green
secrets ambition.
        Consider the absence
        of the gargantuan terrier.

America

I am more and more convinced of American
morbidity. Of their acquaintance,
I convince more Americans that I am more
and more repulsed. As time passes, they begin to like this
about me, that I like that they like repulsion as time passes.
Where might repulsion go? cries 'maltreatment'.

Ten great families fill these lands, we here second cousins;
fascinated with each other's biographies, in the ooze
or quicksand our return to shore is attractively lifeless,
mannikinish. Something about today reminds me of WWI poetry.
Allow me to name WWI poetry
    'The Seriousness of Defenestration's Corpse.'

America is regaining their WWI in poetry, who am I to say
BODY-BODY BODY CAIRN, speak of ethical austerity and the
statistics of post-traumatic stress disorder?
    Hail Affidavit Membership Fee.
I don't even have the right camera to take all your shorthand down.
Luckless, I want everyone to be waiting for me when I arrive home,
since home is my mother. My mother is America,
I want America to be waiting for me when I arrive, Mum.
I want Mom to be waiting for me when I arrive in America.
There is a Daily Show stress disorder affidavit where we laugh,
but the Cadillac we purchase overseas seats five of the best
    body parts.

Stephen Colbert is the murdered president wearing a mask
at a luncheon with the current president, Cadillac Face Spooks.

Laughter, will I ever get this article about the frontline skirmishes
of this recuperation of WWI done?
    I keep getting stuck on soldiers as I saw them: uterine.

Crack shot Reserves take out Friendlies, photograph
the bodies unidentified, send the poems home to their wives
and lovers awaiting. This is nothing like Hiroo Onoda
still at war in the Philippines. Americans are the contrary.
They as yet do not know, however persistent, when it is the
    war begins.

Or, the Whale

The defter eyeglass retracts from prosthesis to close as the lens.
I'm glad we saw the Transit of Venus contraption together.
Today, the toads of the housewarming totter about like a
    hospital gown,
don't they.

Downing Street, fed the car we've become, stripling swerve
at the Royal Close portion that begs greatest
irreverence to hand-eye coordination slovenly. There,
the adverb tourist cum arsonist, it looks as if tradies absence
this time the foundations are here proclaiming divulge;
hello balcony lower jaw!

Perth's scrapers are shaved smooth. Visualise a smashing pug.
No gnashers Tasmania knows nothing of now that it's our donger
on retreat, the gloating *inter festal*.
The arcade turned inside out is the cubicle. Before carburettors,
the steelworks of Wales. They rationed, we start curing our hocks

seawater steeped until the barnacles start their debate
on Father Mapple Gregory Peck versus Father Mapple Orson Welles.
O Delilah, O Deliria! Dialect ornithology
of the charlatan. Left to pass time on this vile rock,
left to grab the roiling wheel as starboard the variorum abnegates
new variorum, floor to the still unrenovated floor
to the front bar of The Clyde.

Adaptation in tempest, adaptation in tempest *in toto*.
Look at charisma under terrific pelt, steam blows off you
like you're fleshless.
The best part about this getaway car waylaid is that I can't fool
any one of you. In comparison, the toads of the housewarming totter
about like a hospital gown, don't they. Hospitable lube.
If only you'd seen the peach groves of Bickley, and below
the tennis court oath.
After all, membership fees kick in by the time of posterity,
and by that stage we all maculate the incumbent planet
which swallowed ours

and called the planetary 'Continental'. That pun looks splendid
unmoved,
must quote Spiderman to F— again. 'With great power comes _____.'
Great responsibility, But.   From mud,
as when spirits get their conjugality with verse and not scriveners
of Law, as for the Abyssinian, my name too is mud, is how it is.

Black Swans

A meeting with white hair today is said to be lunacy.
Blue swimming pools murmur unknowing. Not knowing
a thing about albumen, yolk.
White hair struts atop a pulled Swede turnip. Your black soil
fertile like August, this rosella of science can fluctuate
between Harvard and New York City, even wading through
the swamps.

The same playlist from 2004 clutches your ears
as ears clutch nix, which is their custom! Beckoned back to
        indecision,
not to be spoken to, speak avidly instead to white hair.
'Blue nightingales, for example, intimate to and then retain you.'
Now, however, black swans are no longer indigenous to Perth.
They throttle the fold of your ear, tear it. Nostalgic forgery Exeter
is a lesson.

Breaststroke through swampland, it could all have been swampland
were it not for the hermit on the roof of a hut and the hard
and silent sea. Stranded anaemia, swinging dumbbells of glass,
waving to nobody, this flotsam;
as if on a train metropolis outbound, anaemia's umbilicus
being an earphone between ear and quaking earth.
A deaf memorial awaits his hearing's return to the heat amongst
the pampas and its whistle.

The Body of Bodies of the Body Bodies

The sky is what we apologise for as the undeniable ecumenical
and I like the new windfall, risen heretofore like totality to the flea.
And you say hydroponics are possible anyplace,
so start your buffalo tomatoes in parliament.
That paisley tie and the houndstooth moiety, those who read
Transnistria closely do not necessarily ferry from polity to métier,
something certainly is not up, not wanting
nor harbouring the cat burglar in their closet, though an actor
may be making Tennyson of cloaked darkness. So then,
agreed, say it is sky from which the bullet flies, Acéphale.

My thoughts were to hang the contorted scowl of nabbed Poe
on the wall above the landing and investigate the salt of his earth.
The white desert is purest furthest, flung-set like
the roll of the dice or feline plummet. To think they shortened
the lemon tree so that it'd stop producing citrus.
One man's ocean liner is another man's King James Bible
with the Song of Songs of Song of Songs of Song of Songs
of Song of Songs of Song of Songs of Solomon
torn out. The thoughts that have exhausted you
which morass contains, hides from the third procurement,
from the smoothed brow, turning back the hair and letting sweat
dribble as if from the anxious vein throbbing
like the world of sighs or peristaltic event, or you-know-what
in the gape of the orange of the bird of paradise
purged but for purgatorial

High Wycombe secured in reticulation. To finish
with a conjunction would be worth the pelting of the lead brigade
by members of economist corner, by the economist of the economists
of economist corner, for the economist of the economists of
        economist corner,
had they the squinty eye of all genius, woman in daffodil
lips like a rosebud, puckered at her pregnant husband in brown
turned to the tree lopper in overalls shammed by
the sawdust of spruce.
Thus it is sky we apologise for and why we
fondle alone in night hours when sin is concealed,
or at least the drowning staged at the wreck
of the HMS Orange. Look into the orifice of Da Vinci,
the riddle is a skull not another body, nor another body
of bodies of the body bodies, nor by the body of bodies
of the body bodies, nor for the body of bodies of
the body bodies.

Behemoth's Leviathan

1.
Memories of unconsummated satisfaction in the company of silence
write Aguirre, prince of picaresque moult.
Sat on books – the library was a joke's rotunda – all gaud, slobber;
the slab-backed man with invisible crown
on the covers, white hair mended but matted nearby the self
 portrait of,
gathers his people about him to patronise
Rembrandt van Rijn. They picked for lint and I saw a tooth pounce
from the steam room of the rafty jungle.
To wine,
'There was once a leviathan that ferried their belongings.
It, along with himself. To pour his sinews about…
but those days are dead,' lingers the puckered skin struggling to,
as an example for the others, in turn,
unfurl a book jacket, feeling for a memory. But nothing comes,
 your mother
sutures their tendons true in ligature. With the hope of
poll's request for another slice of lemon in her tea on the
 anniversary of Celan's
being ligaments, one and all. Watch his back,
mother's passing. An inexcusable cruelty of words, indeed,
 look yonder,
stretching too far, chin too high, the small of the back,
'here is Barton Valley. Look up to it, and be tranquil if you can.'
his centre of balance, toppling by the lead
caveat or directive. The passing is a typhoon, that ruins

of hubris, the thick chest pointing toward the potato crop – was the
    flood of Kent
in 2007 an involuntary memory? – the nipples towards
that vague decussation, starting a famine. And that is why we sit here
chatting of reference, pointing towards the most
with an Irishman. Man, he dances. Plaster shakes from his
    brown hair,
impenetrable thicket. A sketch in it
as he abuses all acquaintance with his close-quarter convulsions
of look and torso.
This is nothing like the Schiller Theater Werkstatt, nor am I
    better placed
to adopt that stance and that throne-coloured
judge, to enjoy secrets opulent in lieu having witnessed his
    enthusiasm before.
Glaucous and sinuous. 'We're here to make
even the visiting Californian investment banker in our company
ligaments,' he declares, the second line
thinks, as he empties his pockets the dancer from his hometown.
Of a couplet rhyming with a bated first:
San Diego. Yes, the parlance learnt was first gathered up as
    it scattered
the chest leaden, laden. He leans backwards, sways, he is about,
like coins. However, the Supreme Court-like parade at the
the chin is pointed towards his rapt audience of men,
moment of his nudity let nothing from their mouths but slaver.
The crown is gold vapour. 'What
responded in a wrinkled pucker, but that was all. Rembrandt's stare,

you say?' he cried into the green mist,
shot laser beams into the brains of the company. That was good,
as the barrel chest topples from the raft into the river.
That leviathan memory of belongings is still in port though. Amongst
those of the river is a pail
of their drivel, and one accomplishment: it did eventually become
        apparent to them,
viridian of starvation, the river's rush is inedible.
That the Irishman is the best plasterer in the state of Victoria,
like a statue, of a rigid posture,
you'd do better to come to our next party,
the final gasp. He drops to the bottom of the river an empty.

2.

Steep descent home through concrete and the material
filigreed in the rocks of the foothill plains, these the hieroglyphs
in dirt, emergent palaces on the slope, though a shattered white
of that road to Adelaide once dreamt, the hole in that van's
pane slanted at edge of derision. Somewhere the burbling
that tintinnabulates with proof of the act like a bugle refrain:
all markings of a brick cutter, a truck shudders around the bend,
like these mattoid shakes you have me in. In motion, all is the caul
of the tray of the ute some branches fall in, still embedded
what I become, a cowl I might wear if I contemplated betrayal
at the barrier, comatose and curled like a millipede. A fire,
but now rather just departing. Melbourne cowed behind like
        Melbourne's Melbourne.
Lingers beyond the precipice of the developing mansion's perch,

the coward aflame asleep on the inner gyre of black cloud held aloft
in the dead brush of golden wattle, the brocades of
the season of ash and char, and so piercingly in focus, somehow,
bottlebrush seeds discharging like poppers.
The mallees of this departure on another, as it were, Honour Avenue.
All the xanthorreas are faced toward the cityscape,
exhibiting callow figure the *eirôn* metamorphosed of motion,
        the sullen
urban yeoman nescient of the house held to the bosom of the cliff,
who fasts on the gerbil's wheel and dances the mouse traps in
conversation the boy in uniform salivates at.
Upstream, portraiture of glacier. Fondling the budgerigar behind
all the bower pageant shrieks and shudders transforming into
        plane trees;
the head a huddle of cottages in collapse. The boy sees his
plane trees hooped about the heartstrings of Prahran and St Kilda,
the electron gun colours in the new lights of the nearby slopes,
and the hanging lanterns that Oxford tendered UWA made
and makes of the starling courtship unknown
to the magpies for the workers to continue at night pursued on
the upslope mansion.
Those dramas of Harold Pinter's concrete driveway have furrows
like his father's forehead. He would where John Hurt returns...
The bruited by the brio of a sand plain that I've divorced
would like to share the parental cup of tea, stands to reason bequest
of decisive betrayal, the escort to resentment, propitious if a
        daughter's request
for a rat taught the erect and unmelted glacier. An invitation,

but a daughter's rat bloated in death supervised by the bush mice
that with it once competed. Implacable, the mood with her
and midday near Astor's catharsis. No parents inhabit the hardly-lit
lounge or the cold for their portion of fence-line,
the weatherboard-like asbestos for which I still wipe the linoleum
of the seething temporary life of the kitchen where the vacuum
is the silent, my hands askance, so infertile the threat,
though it would swallow the ashen aromas had it impetus.
Taking the verge unnerved cloaked under umbra's resentment
that strikes you, an image of one doesn't swim in baths of smoke.

3.

Hut in wood, statements of ontology of which Beckett conferences
are black panthers roaming, but not valid currency. The hut cups
the droplets of stardust of a hundred starlings, black ant milk
to fame honey. The undergrowth, awaiting one panther tear
from the gutter, no go the slow tow of closet clay warriors
and their Sarkozy sashes. Slip into your tea cup for trickling water,
and you've found it, viz. sophism's ghost. 'If thou art privy to thy
country's fate, which, happily, foreknowing may avoid, O, speak!'
Suppose this:

found, the hut in a woodland with blood of thumb, blood of hand
blood of nail, blood of hammer, the salmon by the neck,
rattan 2x4s make up the hut's flesh, and fallen off like a cloister. In
comparison,
Tasmania's salmon? Magic whiskey, cured meats of arcana, bollocks
of Merino.

Its inner shell is a window frame, my hands in her hands again.
The contours of nowhere, our fate!
The crime of the sand lot, and consequently the view. Slope of seriousness begun,
so history opens. Soaked in moisture, you hear of landslides here.
Parses the heat of this country, this declaration itself
careful of passion near the slot window, the pane smeared dun
with the history of panthers licking the thumb, notebook of
        Salzburg treatise paradise
crime and so lengthen the pizzle we call knowing and every brick is a window's adversary. And Heidelberg,
that bunker of pistol hiss, panthers ripping up the daisy patch in the lawn, are you the mystery of salt?
In the valley, there sits the open office of salt in stampede
across the clay-mud plain. In a tower nearby the old university
discovering for the first time the singer whose refrain is tossing
the unsent publications the noblest sleep lets lie.
Opening out onto the anonymity of the street, the pedestrian's head inland like a plucked carcass. Truths bled of institution's braces! The hand-spun bowtie of the union!
Of the concave mien we are agreed, perhaps someone like
the person endangered the lyrebirds in an abundance of grasses.
To be believed the plausibility begun as a scapegoat trophy
bearing the moisture that makes the country retreat smell grassier.
But of that thrust knife parses the tide that is foreign to land
diverted, is of paper drifting like a landing aeroplane.
Should have read his face in the trough, and the groans that loom
now recollecting periodical's renaissance at the gash in embargo.

Time has aged the solar invitation,
and time is evidence of imperfect children.

4.
Announcement of the lottery number cues the purloined, the bode
that perishes well,
bush deep as the wattle. To look forward to subpoenas at a distance
now as a border
supplicates that which betrays up to her waist in water, bobbing
then diving,
feeling with her toes the diurnal, plashes of the soaks near of which
she beloved
the sign of the developing telethon, making the face a cleft
proposal, to cow
and recapitulate, she now Eurydice whose portrait the omnibus of a
nation's
pressing on apes. Yes, could be medusoid
had I not known that she'd turned aside for good, and his voice is
just as bashful
on the telephone. Our charity happily stirs, with an absolute and
sober intention,

because I become them, these southern cliffs, having invoked
formulaic calculations of Tetragrammaton being salt and stone
betraying
the news in an itched neck whose hives like, either way, being
looked after.

The full extent of a bulldust sandstorm percolates Sydney's
turning russet
as if in the company of this bespoke version bereaved the
lofty skyline.
As it waits, resented, the company of the choreic flora called
the passions
imagined. Burnt of thaumaturgy, the escape of incident
austerity toward
and abstinence from the event is starting its cocky putrefaction.

Act, rock of Cornwall, comb the locks and the tiger pants
having an affair,
coastal fireworks if to be done with the currents of a chorus
drains the character
of a now second state enlightenment, availing ourselves the
bid farewell
red glower of the first state of entitlement, the rejoinder
called westward.
Yes, the blubber of hives doesn't know what to do either.
A music box
twinkle, the trapped ballet dancer ever vibrating of the saline
appearance
Mornington Peninsula, *pace* the Cornish coast.

Of exacerbation expends the firebrand called the hazard lights,
to have furthered the furthest just found in your leopard skin
now turned palely mine. The gold standard beached,
it really has been but hours incommensurable

with global markets, in shadow of the purloined, the bode
that perishes well, bush-deep as the wattle.
Greyish pediment sat the reflexive moon masking the
burden of the sun, the ague of flares. Night terrors
of chattering austerity. Periodical and appalling men of papers
proceed as we renew the due to continue.

Set Sopor

Albert Tucker's Fitzroy

To sit on a milker's stool in the entry to your cottage
with the fallen carnations and Fitzroy's bitumen smell
rising like a cordon between your disposal and your neighbours.
Here we are in fame state.
You turn the man in mustard trenchcoat away unmoving,
an interrogation on your constancy in this place
of a mode, this tableau of the spectres of Fitzroy lighting
their swollen heads lifted from the gutters
to haunt and doorknock once more. And would trams stop?
The storm of yesterday evening split the beech
at the edge of the garden beds, its slag remains,
bar the black stick, a vermiculate wool blanket and sparrow fluff.
Some are left that chirp above in the alcove
between gable and outside; frozen, you turn the man in mustard
trenchcoat away, but managing to snag his shoelaces
which tangle through the hodgepodge of the sentinel's station.
You're an ankle-snapping dog in lieu of impound leaving its catch
to blanch and encrust in the sun. Little wants burial.
Your mother says you look like a whale carcass, though to hear her
would mean to hear her over the din of Radio Fassbinder,
colluding where gas colludes,
replying where those whose abidance of silence is not revolutionary.
From the radio ebbs a number of places confirming your stool
before the front stoop, deaf to the fall of carnations
and the rising mists of roadwork.

Bobtail

Crouched, thumb and forefinger raised
as pincers, the bobtail is recovered from
an encrusted pool. Evisceration
surreptitious till now,
a tiny tuxedo of skin. Had the pool been familiar,
you'd have done more than leave it
on the lip, the place from which England
sat clutching, the Aussie sun
holiday as hypnotism.
A gangplank awaiting you on the other
ambit now junked over the precipice into
the native brambles, xanthorrhoea, sea-mine-like
wattle blossoms, and a wad of granite boulders
harbouring bauxite. These were the days of sunblind
wealth, haunting the vinyl-covered
settees and polished white tiles,
property of amorphous acquaintances.
You and uncle are parallel, his glad face
wilfully empty, yours dazzled by a wall of
twinkling blue glass in the lounge, souvenirs
from every possible hiding place in the world.
Those who let us through have left,
now that the world has filled with persons.
Arcade shutters are bolted at the floor,
magpies trill as if irreversible morning.
Expressed as such means I'm scorned as you.

Where once the imaginary escape of
a midday bushfire as utes about collide with her,
walking the Zig Zag together you and I discover,
having walked this gift of the plank and survived
puncturing the blue meniscus a second time,
there are thousands idle, some with walking sticks,
some with packs, some arm-in-arm with companion.
At the heated pool, you sit shirtless on the lip of
the trembling water, disturbed by the dozen lappers.
Nothing in the sun before the steam mesmerises you,
either too diffuse or too far away. Fuck knows.
There has not been a day you have basked
in acquaintance since dashing on the slaty declension
of Gooseberry Hill Road. Your interview
with acquaintance's son in an empty, grey-carpeted room,
sun-dulled by portholes of stained glass,
was your last introduction to brass. Swimming pool
disowned today by acquaintance known unknown.

The Black Truck

Before they force me to commit suicide from the
mantle of this hotel's rooftop I should warn you how near
the inner howling contest of the anonymous black
semi-trailer is, what havoc eventuates of an exhibition relay.
No one presumes they might see them, rumours
tell us they supply the occlusion of noise during
a systematic undressing of women scopophilic.
It's some kind of laughing broth they bodyguard at The Europe
Hotel. Discover their spectral impressions in the carpeting,
imagine the shouting match is over, and assume that the truck
ceases its approach. These are techniques for overcoming
what is otherwise too hard to tell for the moment, too elusive
for regular meditation, a single grain to your pitchfork.
Not the name I would have called it, *The Western Limits*.
Something about the wild azalea that draws
an audience about it, chuckling. Some of them smoke.
The hay bale is another way to slow the charge of the singing
tractor, whose farmers enforce silence at home
during drinking hours.

Like the palm of the nationalist, covering his mouth, fondling
        a paper
clip; approaching is master of such a mirage, and the face
he wears when struck dumb before
a nude is the same he commands leering at the cul-de-sac
of his memory of the western limits.

Does the mouth of the palm clutch its viewer?
Need you be afraid?
By the same hand, might you be put to sleep
in the sand before the agapanthus? Some project it in journal,
no prints to the big hand, that's what's horrifying.

That Part in Basquiat When David Bowie Playing Andy Warhol Says

D.H. Lawrence's Bolsheviks are from Hull, from Sheffield,
from the jaundiced liveries of the sulphur carcass sparkling
like a Jubilee. Why is it the Bolsheviks have the eyes of fish.
See: Sergei Eisenstein, Yevgeny Yevtushenko.
Why do all the poets have fish eyes, and tails of caviar
skein. What is it in the semen
of the Bolsheviks that makes light work. Why is it the Queen
unashamedly takes the sartorial Poseidon, does that make
the Queen a scallop. Does that make the Queen Aphrodite.
Does that make this poem a whirling cherub.

Why is it Vladimir Mayakovsky shot himself
through the fish eye. Why is it Ivan the Terrible's dark locks
during the fall start to take on the appearance of the kelp wood,
a weltering memento mori of the sundered and shivering,
shocked and aground hull of the Battleship Potemkin. How is it
the speech falls like rum from the Soviet sailor or soldier's mouth,
as if it were the second best thing to a bowl of unshelled maggots.
How is it speeches come easily at all. I read somewhere that we
are too stupid for speeches; why is that, why are we too stupid for
speeches. Why is it these dreams above ground consist for the most
part of drowning housing estates, and not drowning lovers.
Why is it this nightmare ad infinitum if I were to choose one
of the 'manly' nightly horrors is one who resembles these fish eyes
dropping like a stone to intricately paved red brick, dropping

into the bed of nails, dropping into aeroplane carcass, dropping
like dead lead into wet lead, dropping like wet lead on to dead lead,
from lea to bed to lea to lead ad infinitum.

Why is the Queen a scallop, and why the nacre a
propositional reflection of something other than
the hull of a battleship.
Why is 1916 a poem and not just a holiday, an armistice, an orgy.
Why caviar skeins betwixt each of these brick
fortresses lined with plastic and chewing gum – like our night
on Little Bourke Street and your companionship, except we knew
it to be established on a bed purled of a dozen generations –
why otherwise invisible. Why a burger with the lot, beetroot, egg,
shredded lettuce, bacon, two slices of cheese, dollops of sauce,
condom-like tomato, at 3am. Is this what they call
intent to replace breakfast. And what would the salmon who dresses
her universal waterway for a leap into a higher echelon, the eel
who leaves all her young to be fertilised by another in that one
clean pocket of the spillway from a neighbouring sluice drain,
what would they feel about nacre, about the nudity of steel
in public waters. Public waters with sauce and beer, public waters
of greasy and thinning hair, public waters of the carcasses of sulphur,

'I can't even see what's good anymore.'

No Head for Old Boardwalks

Question time in broad country,
this is no head for old boardwalks,
considering the hinterland cottage and the fifteen
major ancestors and someone's designs
to be emissary.
One lobe then of a bicameral bush trail
that eventuates in the desert,
like the sweaty pub in Toodyay,
or the bush mouth at Kalamunda's peak.
No head to stirrup or give the bit, rummaging
through heirloom trunks for unfilled postcards,
though tarnished brooches with profiles of
those other than the faces of ancestors were
uncovered, not to be unexpected,
of brass, lead and pewter.

Abandoned by her caravan, a young woman
is visited by Venus of Willendorf though a library
does not clutch her collar but a coloured knit
scarf, the floating Venus no longer a projection
from an archive of defunction.
Nudity is the embarrassment of both loners,
the woman invites where the Venus departs,
the woman mouths soundlessly where the Venus
stirs sounds of underbrush by the footsteps
of her ephemeral museum.

They say the design capital has stolen her now,
the woman thinks it is her lips mouthing the captions
of lit artefacts and the Rosetta stone floor
of the empty form of a glorious fleet.
Moldavite feet, she now reads the horses aside
the delivery vans with the speed of the tongue,
their pseudo tetanus shots and fleeced
physiotherapists, the hardness of hooves and
the sobriquets that deliver them healthy,
like black caviar or monkey's pride.

A good enough talisman if you're haunted by the artefact
and wish to plunge into the sedge and seek
the coastline of Albany or the eyes that are the sweaty
lights of the museum, having to omit
the facility of the beachcomber Parisian.
Such feet do not deliver you like the fleet rather
crack you like a hardboiled egg, the
question is: does she plunge or does she investigate?

Jarrah floorboards fitted poorly let light and
dust through, she suffers the curator's thinking
eyes the floor beneath him. When it is that the brooch
of the decapitated profile, the gleam of the Moldavite
foot, or the oolite figure are sought by her, the questions
of the attic start their chain dragging and horse reading.
To quote her eisegesis on Melbourne's khaki jacket,
'if I went back to my parent's street, I would find
myself beginning the Bibbulmun track again.'

The Ear Especially

You don't need eschatology to see the finitude
in all this. Cantilever arm of all sweetness,
pinions of every anatomy
in the sinew of its reaching out. And towards
what? The globe is fine corpulence, the flesh
of the ear especially

vigour of sports car on wet May bitumen slighting
the smart bone catacomb. Paris, hello. Where
have you hidden my brother, and Now,
my brother's brotherhood. There is a Southern Californian
song about all of this that eschatology
cannot penetrate. Cease, sweet claw of new day,
digits clammy.

The clay pits. To gasp with hand on back of head,
to be lulled to sleep like the puppet infanta,
side with brother clover and fatten wanton,
lope the lambent disguise if but only in the moment
of finitude. Need not finitude to see the sweetness
in all of this that made eschatologies
unrenewable, when instead,

and we do know this, the fossil only comes twice,
as in: all time under, the all-time no time above.
That grasp, darling hand, park your car, knowing restlessness
and velocity in the woken, in the face.

Success

There are some bloodhounds lost to the east of the olive grove
and the eldest white gums, where the earth is marshy
and all the blue granite turns green by moss. There are those
who aren't afraid of the canines of the poem. 'Don't suck
a lemon – Success.' And the wombat comes out of its hole
with its hands up. And the fox comes out of its hole with
its hands up. And the rabbit comes out of its hole with its
hands up. And the bilby comes out of its hole with its hands up.
And the brown snake comes out of its hole with its hands up.
And the platypus comes out of its hole with its hands up. And
the wolf spider comes out of its hole with its hands up. And
the opossum comes out of its hole with its hands up. And
the fruit bat comes out of its hole with its hands up. And the
Bombala comes out of its hole with its hands up.
The bloodhounds responsible are the poem.
The canines of the bloodhound are soft from the work of Success.
   The milieu is something like the hole coming out of itself, like
      a stony
      nail strip employed by the police to stop done up Valiants
      and tinted Fairlanes.
            By turning the grit of the subterranean are we to
      close off Brunswick Road
            to allow for the dolly of the wolf spider pageant,
      for the dolly of the rabbit pageant,
                  for the dolly of the wombat pageant, for the
      dolly of the brown snake pageant,

for the dolly of the fruit bat pageant, for the dolly of the
        Bombala pageant, videlicet the
pageant of the hole coming out of itself with its hands up
        for the poem
                where the earth is marshy and shaded by the
        eldest white gums
                        and granite glows green with new moss.
        Éclat for those unafraid of the
                                        canines of the poem.

The Brave Vernacular

Consider the pink slip, a demerit, another moment,
Newtown tirelessly flanking us as we speak.
        There was great offence taken in the hall of exhibitions.
Best ignore any constatives or reflective rhetoric, rather
well represented in that laughing stock the portrait of sheep
and crows. Newtown and others better linger hitching at the cliff
face than truckling to empire, though
as far as we know – which is still something in the range of Alan
        Bond
arm-length con-artistry – the yearly catch is still rare enough
and in small enough portions not to alarm the half-eyed clarions
of borders. A flabby teenage arm
wrung of its charge, weight-loss rhetoric spills from a sovereign
administrator whose borrowings recur stale in
the tape deck of his Camry.

Slippery pink, the language of the contract defeats the parents,
orders eviction by their tongue, and a heavy blue draino haze
        blankets
the rows of lavender. So far, the best one can do is read pitchforks.
Then again, the dog walker – the head appearing between her
        abominable
charge of more than just one Cerberus, a modern – manages
the one fated espionage disclosure endowed her,
transmitting the child toward the secret neighbour who only ever
arrives home, never leaves, the same secret neighbour who knows

a charter pilot feeding Calais, courting Christmas Island, flirting the Cook Islands. It needn't be metaphoric, to fly is Iwasaki's brave vernacular.

The Bucking Bronco

This muscular ore is no mechanical bronco of the pub;
there is no leaving the bare back bestriding so soon demanded us
on allocation of the licence.
Thirteen new smelting sites from top to bottom of a nation
have rekindled their promises to lovers lain still enough
we'd thought their flat bellies and tranquil skin unflinching
had meant decease of the parents.
Yes, the regular are flooding Collins Street with coverings like
the cloche or the panama, the boater or the porkpie, just as
John Brack foresaw, to catch sight of some glow suppressed.
Perturbed quiet as the faces crack open with signs of the decease
of the parents, superficies coax pedestrians to palm reading,
the currency Emma carried for deposit at the ANZ half a block
down, beyond Ahab's call to alms.

Of the children's doll named Isabella, dragged by her hair
like Dickens' generation bespoken, golden tufts like laburnum
sprout from its grapefruit head, the throat and torso stuffed with
tuff from the tablelands. We see in this partnership the shadow
of Nolan's Ned, Whiteley's White.
Diabolical bronco entertains. No more painters in the bloody eyes.
Refrain from context, red eyes. Visor brims tucked into the sneaky
afternoon. Pints of platinum. Entertainment.
How many horses power this metal conjurer jolting,
whinnying by dint of hot chanting, displaced bartender
but a grateful grimace. Black Rock beach. Then turncoat conjurer

charges. No spittle. Blackout. From black, rising cloying Montera
a new hat, woven of the impossible feather-soft hair
of the youngest curdled botany, impertinent battler.

Finally, the black pneumatic conjurer throws. Splayed dumbly
with an ersatz throne of disused company, mechanical Grendel now
inert as the captive blackout
all gibbous haunches, faceless as the lid of the Montera endowed us,
the glower of a smouldering night punctures the blackness of the
pub, heads as hatless and nude as Lula's open mouth.
Hadn't we been bequeathed the headdress of the karakul?
Hadn't I been thrown from my mount?
No imitations in the sneaky pub, no accoutrements of the funereal
nearest, sweating in black? Somehow, new currency weighing down
these coat pockets singeing, making the aromas of the forge,
my pockets, they animate, they live.
Lula, your Cadillac never was enough to seduce from distraction,
but hot satellites are finally set alight in honour of the flames and
    what was unfairly
lost for your father,
we make no comparison, brainless caught in the piecemeal throne.

Green hands and curling fingers draw us out of the darkened
rooms and onto the camels that deface portraiture of Australian
episodes. Collins Street evacuates 5pm, we linger late in pursuit,
without discrimination the red night promises affray.

The Character

Something unacknowledged
in that division of waters at Cape Naturaliste,
there is even anonymity of character
in a name's worth.
I wear the memory of she who remembers him
more significantly the more she abstains from his memory,
mnemonics of trembling in murmurs
of sleep on a subject of which she is otherwise mute,
fair enough, healthy concealment, hair draped over
and partitioning vision
and the canola farming beyond the rise of hills.
We set out to tend the risible questions, universities
emptied and ashen, printers the pending with heads bowed
cheese folded into lumps of torn bread. At night,
in an inscrutable desertion she slips into sleep hung
from my neck like a frigate.
On holiday, lassitude in a converted butcher's
now a bistro, to drink beer and coffee. The meat hooks glint
hang your head.
Days never seem to end until he appears, the character,
one with nix for the printers,
shod with the ashes of the institution, but tumult contained,
sewn into his viscera. It's May in Melbourne
and all the fireplaces are attractive,
shimmering eyes of appraisal of separation. The fraternity
revolves in the turnover and it's still May in Melbourne

for the holidaying, the printers proof the currency arrived
from Cape Naturaliste, from Albany to Boyup Brook.
There is all but peace in peacetime, and gilt edges to the dawns
of winter. Character's as big as a horse and she says so,
glad that he does not slide from atop the bascule bridge
or make a speech in the squares or the courtyards.
You mention the slide. The back of my hand gasped during
the drama of the bascule deglutition.
There is something to the absence of whipping this hand, this gasp,
the missing punishment of the corpus,
nightly vigil instead wearing the cap of the dunce. Its history
restrains more than private don, especially from pedagogy.
To hear her speak of him, to hear her admire
the anonymous fiction not slept and of a cautious gladness she has
centres the horse riding proposition,
proposition to survey the lines of equipoise
and poke holes through the canola fields concealment
the gulch in my memory mutes of the character,
of which Cape Naturaliste murmurs of trespass, which settles
scores in susurration,
and divisions and the tasks
of the printers paradise auto-tunes.

Resuscitation of the Dancing Bears Pony, the Commonweal

Ham hock and the union of dancing bears
made redundant, how brash
your squirm on acolyte perm demonstration
indeed! There, we are their here-there,
their there-there shenanigan. Puncture of the coolant,
incontinent enamour of ardour,
when North Carlton ain't North Carlton
much longer anatomising real estate beer price
Great Northern. Within which
suffers infant at breast in the stories,
unbattened Alberta,
gape gape and ginger beer to the masses
that entreat where entreaty

darkly cocoa. Winter. He barters less with his obnoxious
bit, reads more Sylvia Plath. Advisable seasonal Tourette's this,
the *narodnost*. This means marvellous Mitsubishi
Lancer handmedown narcolepsy takes here's doorcharge,
sanctions there's whereabouts catastrophe.
Whereabouts catastrophe having brained acquaintance's

colleague pacing like the Sartrean Bengal tiger
at the wedding. Elsewhere, palliative giants.
Vox populi postal vote. Why else date at the zoo
but to entitle the dress circle prism to demonstrate
gape gait and gait gape pace, to and fro.

Lesbia

Rather than scaffolding the ruins of the waxen
bone pavilion, an obstinate presence,
he has been lost to the speakeasies and restaurants,
where pine unvarnished lingers longer
than the iron shell that encloses the hot interior.
        But how, considers Peggy Guggenheim.
        For whom, asks Flann O'Brien.

Sweet Lesbia, where goes your inquiry during the years
of Melbourne's return to unmaking? Has he betrayed
you, ever longing for your image at the piano,
in the sequins that shimmer in shrieks from the depths
of heavy pleating? The best martini is the barrister's,
but the barrister's yuzu lemons are not in yet,
a heavy bounty of his own gibbous, or 'weeping', in back
of a long miner's cottage backyard by an old foxhole
and a decrepit fuchsia dunny.

The yuzu tree has monopolised its friendships, you do not
see the fox pissing on any other
tree, nor retreating elsewhere as the barrister comes to sit on the
gossamer toilet pretending to be his father.

Bob Hawke, the adulterer, speaks. Suppose then that the
speakeasy's prize and otherwise unemployed bathrobe

the empty skull of Cambridge
when encouraged to return to his sweet Lesbia,

languid wanderer of the rim of Lake Garda, he means to hang
lights from the ruin and, as the dimmer swells to a crescendo,

watch them pop.

Waiting for Minor Dogs by Astrid Lorange

minor dogs dispatch
beyond ken of the fire department
abut Coburg in the crook
of His Honourable's pit, there sure are a lot of Lasers
passing up and down the Bell Street exit

Returning to Anonymous Bay in Shizuoka
its bay-side kiosk shrivelled to a hard kernel
of maize. The trick is to boil its insides

until it pops, rather than pulping it
for some intrinsic bounty. That'd be a big dog
like a tallish Alsatian, minding the ticket gate
to state politician's retreat,

where the acacias shade under willow foolhardiness
a ballyhoo of consolidation if you tend to the whispers
of the rangers under dubious environmental
initiatives to keep what's keeping, tantamount to

burning with sledge, or slag pit dreaming

if you ask the divestitured local fire fighters transferred
to the old post office at valley's edge in Brunswick West
its back end deracinated, nothing but boxes
and idlers, idle boxers, and under rarest sun,

this being 5am with the smaller dogs yapping
The Lasers centrifuge spin at the exit
and whistle for reprisal

you forget once you've popped having
luck at your clavicle and no tickets
asked at entry. The whispers in the pit!
That's sauce resource

or the source resourceful, plonked like a convertible
at the razor wire gate to the quays where
crab fishermen and sea mackerel boaters alike launch
unfed but baying, the sun still

but a hard skin at horizon's mount as they
clean their nails by torchlight

You're Cute Where the Passionfruit Ends and the Neighbours Begin

In fur, the yolk and the pounce test. Hanging your shirts
from the hooks for hanging baskets euphemises
summer afternoon's jokes about the impending action.
Example: the mail would come by hand by person in high visibility

gait the peremptory, your grimace at the trellis of passionfruit vine
and our junked electric heater open at the grill with grey viscera
and wide open mouth otiose,
'how churlishly unwelcome' unhumoured. Has he never heard
of the spider baby or the seldom seen engagement, never seen
murals

of Humphrey Bogart or dried meat hung like pearls. You Wonder.
Cautioned subjects of endanger, the subject to treachery slovenly,
having after all no designated evacuation twain,
rot stench of hung succulents the load of garage letters,
where the passionfruit ends and the neighbours begin.
  The taxation encyclopaedias in shade:

the moult of the missing collie. Tony's bull dog in today, pet him
like a man's head. The absent yolk he ate, one supposes.
No moult, no sign of him now, you would know if a predator
when a predator. Answers, they come at the brink of the act,

act become act-ion. The Any Dog inevitably rolls in after birth, so

should ensue our debate about Marlon Brando.
You forgot you obliged. Sometimes a classroom looks like
a peacock's coiffure, the ostentation of new building contracts built
on the number of cranes on the skyline.

The council had approved yours, but then you hung the gerberas
of the torpid lee. See, the mailman in high vis likes the proportions
to the frontal tableaux. I argue daily with my housemate
over re-establishing the college's pomegranate sapling to the bed
of our front yard – every confidence prudent, would not broach
a pomegranate subject – she is ever reinvoking the realities of
renting, thus the entailed disapprobation remaining.

Grey viscera jingles at night, someone's kicking it in one guesses
but fathomlessly in dream, Rock of Amnesia, lets nothing.
Must be six o'clock again, returned again to permissive Cuba
not to mention its paradoxical chalk-line foreshore also.
Cans rattle there somewhat similarly. Philately, olive oil rivulets
running the meniscus like hanging pearl like rope floats.
Topics of danger reconstitute pleasure's jokes, like that one about
the passionfruit vine and the mailman *a fortiori*.

Bogart's likeness in biltong. You're cute, she says in furs.
Yes, you're sidelined from the patron's bankrolled project to return
for the yolk of Duncan Hose's bullfight to bullfight Duncan Hose.
Barcelona night crawling with sweat, mildewed blinds. The plenary
enthralment, spittle-toothed
Bed made of passionfruit afterthoughts,

who knew the bull dog made up the yolk and left smidgen
afterthought. After Cuba, well good luck to you. The mailman
is outspoken when he can be but leaves no moult, effectively no
sign of him. Taxation encyclopaedias bear their prize,
in the eucalypt calm, desuetude of severest sight.

So, a house with egg on its face is highest competition.

Like a Prodigal

Of import substantial dull. Claim to the archipelago,
and here we mean the tilt of Oceania,
the corpus of the runny particulars of the Philippines
as outpost to rim is rudimentary geology. Outpost of rim

can mean a role in adoption. Volcanic lips were cool
when he first claimed us as parents, roughage emesis
necessary when roughage sets to claim
Queen and country, and so asks, and quickly,

where the national's been foraging. Verdant inheritance.
Does 'Glorious Mystery' claim same dullard as opposite,
opposed to principles of the molten? Of callousness,
freight train Thomas De Quincey, the proper audacity.
Adequate
archipelago on Gertrude Street at 1am, from which
you see the billboard

but no one else but the same 'you' rotten
simpering from Yah Yah's with a pie mouthful.
Someone's icon of Mao similarly masticating but gleaming.
Go, glower after gravy. But, do you glow after gravy?

We are fine parents, but inarticulate; nostalgic after all
of trams that do not bolt but creak stentorian.
'...or who the herald...'

Fire at Easey Street, someone's paperbark assumed sacrifice
necessitated when in bloom, whose tiny gold blossoms
zip galvanised starlit on mope morning.

Canned skulls, you remember, I hope, the shipment
for the protection of food in aspic Revolutionary projects.

Once the glare of Queen and Country, then
the locomotion of the modern – the retina will mist
eventually at speed – to rest, for now,
with those working to work. There's no blood yet
in this new child of ours' lips.

'Canned bread!' he suffers. 'Canned bread!' exclamations
when it's we ate the eggs.
Adoption of the similar has bated the gullet of the young
wanting residence sun bask,
we give him food the new century sod but he'll spit
all over the plate like a prodigal, the prodigal prodigal.

Night's Mitre

At dusk, departing like a bandicoot
or a jogger. Would not sing to
Northern Ireland if Northern Ireland
did not sing to you. The proposal
of gin, marriage. Park Street hides
a livid priest and two regal transvestites.
Wear red to distract from the dead
car, where in it lay the escapade. But,
no longer inheres the escapade.

Hungry is the thin loam of outskirt Victoria,
you touch her cheek but until arrival
let her sleep, the closed mouth concealing
all the insides, like black rain.
Could that have been the outcome of
the levelling of the isolated island scurfy
with silver grass and samphire and the stretched
corpses of the seagulls?
Pelican swallows seagull, seagull swallows mussel,
mussel swallows barnacle, barnacle swallows
the hourglass. The hourglass
turns with the finished island now
frothy with ocean. The car that is a mouth,
shut up with all its iron keys and rattan styrofoam.
The red attendant supervising the minor
giant feels for some sign in the dead chassis but

none of this landscape moves but the odious
maws of gulls.

To thrust car to sea
begets youth's memory of tapered cardigans
and flick-knives and the coast of California,
its breadth and intents James Dean suave,
but we're not here for that, we're here for the fresh-facedness of
youth caught by surprise in greens and greys,
like the anxious subjects of Leonardo Da Vinci.

It is night in the island froth of her gall.

Walk the Plank!

There are none that write his biography, but a committee mounts
anyhow. They meet tomorrow. Crucial spasms beaten by the
mandarin that rolls weary. And then there is the Pelham Street
renaissance, a Justin Clemens appearance,
new offices, and beaten tracks no country for old Byzantium.
They meet tomorrow. These fascicles and the Catholic incense
on the balcony, clinging to the cheeks of the newborn that intends.
Leave it there, Joy, until the arrival of plant life, myrrh,
the bells of skunk cabbage furled, the birds of paradise.
Defence as the *torii* of a gladly forgotten sharehouse. Baffled
terrorista in tow. The lungs of a new civil war:
and have you considered how many tonnes you filter for the benefit?
Crucial spasms beaten by a cult of Queensland that roams
but cavils. There, I just saw dialectics, the muse.
Who might she be that turns her head from the Grampians
introduction, the headline presumption, toward communal bathing?
Because tuberculosis is a pathogen still in the puddles of Montana
or sacred lost Toodyay, which hides its kayaks during the bushfire I
was absent for. Bereft as usual its clearings and the dog leashed.
Shame, I must catch up with her on the road, and then her again
in cameo, and then, beautiful question and progenitor
of the communal bath, in disguise, walking the plank of the loiter,
walking the plank of the highway's shoulder,
to whisper in her museless ear.

Brando to Brando, Headboard of Headboard

To start vainly, that was his conduct about the pantry moths
and the waking rheumatic poltergeist, but who even believes in
LA, or love of the cornea? Densely believable,
like the account of white beards, presumably, ebulliently
unperturbed, even, Burroughs or Brautigan, the pupil barney
or gurney, because all is wedded 'to be'. And decent eyes about
the letters of Hollywood, Brando to Williams, Brando to Brando.
Stella Adler the News, the remittance notice, not unlike
the doorknocking; the tax office did refund me for some past
transgression of an historical university floated now on inner tubes
and the deglutitional lubricant. Starting vainly, the dreaming
splatters a shot pellet of grimoires on the headboard of dreams
become headboard of headboard.

Yemeni ogives in tassels: what grandparents they had been
intended before becoming sloth grandparents. The prigs of spelling
they've become in vain, gagging on the minutest thorny
substantive. The nightingale legs of the night owl,
could he but Benjamin his way into a full revolution of the neck
to look all the way around at this minuscule moment in time
where the grandparents push our German concatenations around
like jigsaw pieces and the dreamer can submit
to hermitage without molestation.

The hurdler lifts himself vainly from the bed like a girdle.

Risen Temples

Yes, the trompe l'oeil Tsurugidake and the wanton
    scattering we make looking
for its haze and shrapnel between our toes.
Yes, anthems that are vigilante announcements in
    unmarked cars and balaclavas.
Yes, Tsurugidake standing as a cut-out, of sky, of sky
    upended, of sky stabbed cuneiform
into the skull of the earth, to stand erect and immovable like
    the Mayan temple deposed
to the deferred thicket, the inert basin.
Yes, the darting girl running across town barefoot to meet
    the phlegmatic historian.
Yes, after visiting her temple, combing the hair from her
    cheek, she awakens, turns back the sheet.
Yes, between us and a weekend template is the Corolla's
    insentience, glistening like
the find of the big toenail in Princes Park intact.
Yes, both their hair is white and they smile toothily, like
    abalone.
Yes, the unrecited anthem sounds rather like the tone of
    your mother's voice sounding like
the mosaic crack at the end of *Wozzeck's* Marie's *Sprechgesang*
    in the kitchen, or rather like
the contraction of ice.
Yes, both their hair is white and he tugs at her as to a nun
    of Western Australia,

outlining with long fingers of the left hand there hovers
    a red aureole
like the caps of the temple icons of Toyama and
    elsewhere though her aureole sconced
in the wheat belt knows no geography but the active
    microbes called leavening agents,
whose risen temples are accidents.
Yes, the darting girl must beware maculating her shirt
    and underwear,
the weather is so mercurial and the ground so sodden
    with rising clay and new lodes
best she does not mark her white shoes hence leaving
    those swathes the clogs.
Yes, all along the historian and his mock Dürer or
    speculative Da Vinci sketches,
draughtsmanship of the vagrant grapheme or machine
    part, papering the walls, are their
stars bundled up above and all around, acquiring them
    from the tug of their perfumes.
Yes, she is the shard of no man's land shredding his
    tissues and mocking his
history, bringing his speeches of stammer to the crust,
    best he announce nothing.

Whose Virgil is This?

Purgatory: linoleum ante-room unchanged eye of the storm.
The replacement body straitened like an anvil, the cruise mustered
Like an iron canvas chart, tungsten was the fiat

Head, challenge permitting at the Adventist college.
There is no competition but pride is at stake. To swim where
Rowing supposed, languor the mask in sheaths inverts.
That makes three glorious

Red gums not fleeting.
Mar the berg man fustian on banana palisades,
The bollardry of brain country. Prig with record.

The missing welcome eked by a snuck head
Through the door jamb in a statement
Of tacit meritocracy, heart tell-tale. 'Let the veins of my head in',
The tithe like a knot in lunar seasons,

Vein's junction where the peppermint tree
Lolls transfixed by its occupation,
Meeting point of girls and boys dorms of the interior,
The sun confirms. 'Bivouac next year?'
She asks, like the shrieks of jarrah floorboards,
The kind used to send all tourists wayward.

'They'll wheelbarrow me for sure. Doomed. Set me
For the brick house, will you, while they play
Eighteen holes across the way. You know?' Silence and hot eyes.
'Heard otherwise?'

I Know It, she begrudges, the missing coda to Tristan Tzara's
    'Unmanifesto',
Though the Quaker has it the Unvert

Think tank high-jacked it for leverage at a Vanderbilt University
Conference, Tennessee. The secret snow tied down to VHS tape,

The ur-trash of course the oil that runs the steam. Upton Sinclair,
    The berg convict.
No red gum need seize
The bank since it is the very guts of it, rowers languishing like a
    College,

Happenstance of easiest entertainments. After all, who is Virgil
Here? The sound of sex falling is a fiat. The replacement head
He's mustering,
Like privileging a steel knuckle of Kwinana,
    Is high ignominy,
Hydraulic or otherwise. And if the bowling ball were his head then
Here sutures Charlotte Corday to St John the Baptist!
Perfunctory Americanism: Vacation.

The fracturing of an iron canvas intimates, 'the languor of seasons
On the welded bank is high time,' and to which 'what' the
    Companion
Seethes. 'Who knows what,' means to bow this in magnetic tape;
Writing, and for the fields of old Federation, the autodidact.

Low groan, but further circles of muscle and blot yet. The
    ungainly Monologues

Depart. Here under cruelty they love long in the oil dark.

Didcot Parkway

She is awake but in abatement. See the collected Ashbery
there in her punt, listless as the river draws it downstream behind,
diverts from the blister on her tongue and so maddens,

like coal burning, like Didcot Parkway in the anytime,
Reading suits returned to Oxford decapitation and so the
punctuality of prudence confirmed for the rheumatoid hip.
1987 after all,

see 1981 looking more handsome than 1999. In fact, few knew
shadows exceeded the cave in that shred of medievalism abut
a new Millennium. Though atavism now, then a Centaur would've

been fresh Priapus, swell to the sweetmeat. Where does my
black pudding end? Delphi Delphi Delphi Delphi Delphi Delphi.
The swarms of us cyclists, any city too narrow for confident

cycling is no cup of blood, curt toothsome vile jelly. Here, I miss
the weekly ritual of the skies lanced by hot air balloons
in Parkville, Buckmaster didn't see this, but you do. See, you're
taken with it now,

and when the leer is stoked, all ends. Watch spit dry: watch fire die.
Rapidest leers nosology exhibit in retrospective.
The marvel is still the marvel.

Look here at some parts of my history and the arse cheek goes
numb. They call it the sciatic nerve, I call it *Snakes on a Plane*.
She calls it fill of Delphi, a fill of Delphi *a fortiori*. Assam tea.
Can hardly get you something unrare. Might fell a cypress
on our behalf, for the souvenir.

The Cocktail Party

'the weasel under the cocktail cabinet' – HAROLD PINTER

The weasel under the cocktail party bar cabinet, vibrations
spasmodic in Pandora's Box, the let loose Huntington's disease,
samovar locket when burst sear the private perfumes.
Werner Herzog returns his nuns to their pontiff,
a mystery play slays the disease herd, ripe between the eyes,
right between the eyes. Those mystery plays
do still educate, and if only she knew, she'd gloat in an
instant. Secret dice town, show us your hand.
Sorrel kept him going, between the transport of the box
and the introduction to the doctor's family,
but nothing fleshy, nor fleshly, nor flesh at all.

Plenty of noise made in the transport and some thought
fulguration doses harmful to the summer breeze,
but that's all in the past now. The Blue Mountains something
else entirely when you think of the Jim Carroll Band,
and just how long we've been waiting for our plaintive chicken
wire stage like union hall like boxing ring refrain
the wading pond like Hampstead for members only
for at least twenty two years, the turn coming sometime
around then. And the run, the run dry, the runner dryly, the runt
driest running for Collingwood, where the archives
were stave stowed, that's worth getting admin funk for,

if funk is meant as stench at driest mouth of the corpus
fealty frozen to the console where the droop,
thus the drop, is made.

Tannic soap ran briskly over the jape town where reason
gave futures, futures made together
teased in troth the wake to the run dry in fact made room
for the runt driest running dryly for the autumn cool
and under patronage of boredom slalom to the new fall.
You were the best and so still you appear considered
understood as troth done fulsomely dutifully,
how might any take your arm from around their neck
when plangent from the teeth sounds your sibilance called
seasonality has mesmerised their bridge between the eyes
thus our between the eyes.

Hours. And the hourly sprain to the cantilever bridge but still
pertaining to the world's supremest. But then gracefully
silly appears that education, and the cocktail kind of monopolises
that conversation on making play of the plume sort,
the true saltation, the sort the true makes the sprain skerrick
terrain of. Each foot flummoxed the train line jarrah,
and so impersonated the island. That might be best then
for the coming masquerade, when the Spanish knight drifts
into the Pilbara and finds Sophocles instead in the pastoral
instead of the prod. Her weasels wild returning?
Wild returning weasels her.

Well, that would make sense were there not animals between
their respective literary circles: for one circle, cotton wool is for
dabbing the pus of the infected, for the other it is for projects of
taxidermy.

Is no benevolent harrier in of our midst, or cinema usher,
circulating mobile film spool collection? Might your mouth be
stuffed with celluloid, or is the pus pressing and demanding of
understudies, the playwright caucus and parties? More martinis,
more whiskeys, more sweating and congealing olives impaled like
the adversary's heads' enemies!

The Pandora's Box weeps, having left the tetter trail
of rotten and fraudulent receipts, for Her Majesty included,
one of which folded in her image. What a shame,
since the torment has in a sense been displaced to some other
sorry territory like the white hotel, surely sou'westerly
ensconced. Glad to see rabid foam flush the pap, though,
much respected by the swine herd and his ulteriority of sheep.

Birth begun proved dangerous to the birthed, but natural
to birth the borne berth burr the breadth of birth,
because the breadth of birth must by nature engender all
things in retrospect a kind of treachery, or seem to,
and so the weasel must be mad and we must survive it
to assay it and draw compunction from our humanity stench.

'The trenches' the wittiest of the handsome but entailed throng
of the vault torch the flaunt fort the appreciation society
of the impossible locket has said previously. Don't mind that.
You don't see that stopping any from raising this bullet
from its pulpit the soapbox stove rostrum, and nor should it,
the weasel might just fall from it, and from it fall the perfumes
of the contents of those olives, all the snakes and the songs to those
snakes it once
mesmerised into dance and parried.
Drive dissatisfaction the highways home and you are incensed
undreamy countermand to all that gin so seared
the undivided acolytes and so prodded their once mystery play
like treacheries into a cajole of nature the cornea myth.

The runner, he didn't look once at the torment of his hands,
like hands drifting over the arabesques in the cornices
of that cocktail party. Though he might be pariah, of the deserts,
there came upon him the taint, one for all recognition,
one and all, and the future like a vault opened up at his feet,
troth toasting called party crashing the gloam

of the mask that appears also a junk samovar covered in prints
The doctor's family are forced to bear all this the guest who stains
its equanimity with recollections of the Lazar house
subjects a family encased in privet and the cautions
of a specialist. Specialists in? It might never emerge, he keeps
his bathroom tantamount to perfect hygiene.

Swear you hear dice clatter in the en suite, see what he says.
Might someone name the weasel, or would blame turn on unruliest
cocktail party guest, the same who stole the toothpicks, left an
artefact of the act: an individual spur piercing the sole of morning?
Now that I would like to know.